Advance Praise for
ROOTED & RISEN

"Here is a wide-hearted man utterly in love with the ground on which he stands, with the broad-limbed and leafing trunks, with the antlered powers and the rain-swollen clouds. On some nights his sleep carries him down and down into the earth where he encounters his ancestors; on others, the crescent moon pours an unseen wine into his chest, and he begins to sing. His songs are these poems.

"Timothy P. McLaughlin is an oral poet, and hence the texts written herein are like musical scores; they are meant to be voiced aloud, their rhythms and tones sounded on the breath so they can join the conversation already underway between the thrumming crickets and the coyotes and the wind whooshing through the telephone wires. Yet the clustered words on these pages can also be viewed as cairns—piles of precise stones or terms marking McLaughlin's way into the many-voiced forest, investigating the manner in which human language, by praising, transforms to prayer."
—David Abram, author of *Becoming Animal: An Earthly Cosmology*

"I love this collection—love the soul/heart's evanescence flaking into stanzaic embodiments of bright effervescence to express our oneness, our beauty and fragility; these poems commemorate and celebrate our gratitude, each is a thumb-nail scoop of God's love for us...."
—Jimmy Santiago Baca, author of *Singing at the Gates*

"For poetry to do its magic, there must be evocative space around the poems and also space around the heart and mind of the poet—giving the reader room to move freely, to change, to see anew, to evoke a leap in the heart and an opening of the mind. From the truthful title, to the lovely section headings, to the poems themselves, Timothy P. McLaughlin offers the reader all of the above—and more!"
—Fr. Richard Rohr, author of *Falling Upward: A Spirituality for the Two Halves of Life*

"I am honored to express my support for this very meaningful book of poems. With this work, Timothy P. McLaughlin beautifully shares his vision of our planet. For many years, he lived among indigenous people, particularly the Lakota, and has participated in our cultural traditions with deep respect and great integrity. His writing reflects his devotion to the Lakota way of living in harmony and communication with all forms of life. *Mitakuye Oyasin*."
—Basil Brave Heart, Lakota elder and author of *The Spiritual Journey of a Brave Heart*

"These quiet poems take the measure of a man who turns to nature to be instructed on being human. Like Rilke in his apprenticeship with Rodin, they record the struggle first to see, and then to sing the 'tender, fledgling visions.' More than a faithful record of moments of true seeing, the poems can turn into ceremonies, enacting ancient strategies for shedding 'the stale swirl of thought as self' and opening to fresh elemental energies. The book becomes almost a manual on how to go out into the natural world, empty yourself, and listen for 'the pure prayer of pleasure that the Earth sings.' A touching, tender debut."
—Morgan Farley, author of *Name Yourself Feast*

ROOTED
&
RISEN

poems

TIMOTHY P. McLAUGHLIN

HOMEBOUND PUBLICATIONS
Ensuring the Mainstream isn't the Only Stream

Homebound Publications

Ensuring the mainstream isn't the only stream

WWW.HOMEBOUNDPUBLICATIONS.COM

Copyright © 2016 Timothy P. McLaughlin

WWW.HOMEBOUNDPUBLICATIONS.COM

Published in 2016 • Homebound Publications
Cover and Interior Design • Jason Kirkey
Author photograph by Jason S. Ordaz
ISBN • 978-0-9889430-8-7
First Edition Trade Paperback

10 9 8 7 6 5 4 3 2 1

in humble service to the dialogue
between the human spirit and the natural world
in all its forms and flows

Dearest Reader,

*Poetry, as you surely know, is best experienced
in the mouth and ear as well as the mind and
soul. In honor of that truth, I warmly invite you
to intone the poems of this collection aloud as
well as, or even instead of, reading them silently.*

Contents

If we surrendered
to earth's intelligence
we could rise up rooted, like trees.

—RAINER MARIA RILKE
The Book of Hours

ROOTED
&
RISEN

STILL

The Pines

How many times have
the pines
been blown
through
to sound this song,
circling their heads
and fluttering their fingers
in brilliant surrender
to wind
or no wind?

The newer shoots
move shyly,
still not a half hundred
years here,
still imagining
their future limbs and cones
and their space in the sky
and the soil.

The tall dancers
have not a thought
to interrupt
their movements:
whether the sap runs smooth
or gums up,
whether the rains are here
or far from coming,
whether they'll sing today
or hold the silence,
they trust it all,
and seem to be, somehow
smiling.

Even the surveyor's eye
cannot break
their joy,
for the hymns they know,
and have so long repeated,
would echo yet
in the roof beams
or the machine fire
or the termites' endless
chewing.

Feeding the Sun

When I see one thing,
anything—this fallen branch, for instance—
for what it fully is,
there can be only one honest response:
praise. The beauty of it—
manifold yet unsung—a sloping stick
lit up in ribbons of sun, callused by cold wind
and a thousand shallow burials and
resilient new nascences.

And then to have my mute gazing
accompanied by a startle of clear birdsong,
to recall that some things even *sing*
their way in this world: my brimming cup
has more than overflowed, it has burst
into light and flooded back into the Sun:
me feeding him for once, like a child
with a humble morsel in hand, reaching up
to a father's open mouth.

Waiting

I waited and waited a great while
before I knew enough
about listening
to hear the bright ones
speak,
and only faintly at first,
so I wasn't sure if anything
had happened at all.

A long nothing
makes the sudden
something almost too much
to bear. And crashing in
instantly were waves of doubt, swirling,
bubbling about, eager to pull down and
drown my first visitation.

But when I breathed her up—
oh lustrous angel—
by way of my sure spine and
eased eyes, the foam settled
and slid back to tide.
And when I offered her
my next breath,
fluid and sweet, the whole ocean
rang out, an infinitude of
sparks dancing and
glittering in the sunlit swath of sea.

My mind melted
in the wash of that chorus;
various and wild, the notes stung
my heart and seized my chest
like a hook in the flesh—

me the dangling
fish, ready to be filleted and
eaten by the Divine.

And I might have hung
there still, through
a hundred lifetimes, happily captive,
the day my ears
first ceased their vain reaching
and began to blossom
softly inward.

Listening

I'm not entirely sure what occurs
during the deepest sleeps,
but, upon waking,
there's often a hunger humming
and a child running
and a fervent beating, like fly wings,
within my breast.
And beneath all that buzz and bustle
wanting to leap forth,
there's a stillness so complete
that I actually
do not move at all.

Like soaking once more
in the womb waters,
my body desires only
to listen
and so to know
what might truly be speaking
behind the usual voices.
In that pure surrender,
the few stark words can finally
catch flame in my heart
and wind up through my throat
like a honey rising
to warm the tongue.

In those depths,
even the unruly flies
do not dare stir—
everything stands at attention—
ready for me
to turn this swinging breath
into sound,

to burn the left-for-dead air
with a song—
nectar streaming and seeding
the spaces gone dry.

Shadow

To rest my eyes awhile,
these days I'm gazing only at the shadows of things.

After all this well-lit studying of the world, it seems
the sleek silhouettes are what delight me most:
their edges painted soft, their movements pleasantly muted
                                      like sound rippling underwater.

With my own form, the skin's finally just right:
the precise color of light caught in the tight-knit net of flesh,
its glow bleeding kindly around the edges of this old container.

It's so good to see all of me there—not just hands or kneecaps
or the lower bit of chest—but the whole lean dancer
laid out flat on the soil or propped upon a wall.

And then I know better my hollow, porous, and distensible truth:
my breath meandering out in wanderlust then diving back to shelter,
my voice filling a canyon and dissolving into silence,
my eyes touching faraway forests

                             and returning to this protracted late-day shadow
that ventures out to the horizon and is enfolded by waves of darkness:
one a thin sheet spreading slowly from the west, another a great blanket
rising in the east to cover up our Earth for the night.

Storage

It is a simple thought
to say the heart, in a way,
must be quite like an old cellar.

> A space to hold things
> or hold space
> for light or shadow to shine forth.

A place of whole acceptance, cradling all
until filled or overfilled:
boxes stacked and shelves stuffed,
webs and mold and micro worlds
proliferating the unattended darkness.

> To most folks,
> the things feel put away, dealt with,
> yet a burden appears plainly
> in the heavy eyes and heavier steps
> of the attending body.

The cellar can, of course,
be cleaned and cleared, swept out
and lit up,
the stacks slimmed, the files trimmed,
the shelves relieved and lightened.

> The door can be opened to new air,
> a window dug and built
> to permit sunshine and moon glow,
> a song hummed into the bare walls and cold floors.

All that is surely good, it seems:
a refreshment, a warming, an illumination.

It is also good, essential really,
to descend into the storage space
on a moonless night
and feel the crawling and prowling
of animal and spirit,

to stand silently before
the long shut-up boxes on leaning shelves
and simply weep
      until morning or sleep
            sweeps you up and carries you back
                into the comforts
                    of the living room.

Seeking Nothing

You could dwell for days in the space between language
     and no language, between the thing itself and
     the many names for it, between living and the story of it.

Of all the ambling word paths before you, you choose none;
     and yet, you also choose not the unmapped sky above.
     You are nowhere and have said nothing,
     have refused the bait of any line of inquiry.

You will sit. You will fast. You will become the emptiness around you
     until something—who knows what: a stone-bodied angel,
     a woody spirit hand—sees your readiness and comes to lift
     you up beyond the frozen frontiers of your old standing.

That's what it means to be quiet. That's a secret canyon worth your exploration.

Halt all the mind's wheels; scale back your breath to a trickle;
     let your blood become still lakes. Stop looking or listening;
     allow the will to fall aslumber. Go right to the outer edge
     and drop yourself off the precipice into the darkness.

Then you could slip free of old skins to *become* the things you love:
     plump-bellied peaches hanging in glinted, dying sunlight,
     searing green grasshoppers perched bashfully on cannon legs,
     leathery red leaves pasted delicately into wet mud.

For we cannot begin to appreciate life—marvelous knotting
     of shine and shadow—until we have really let go of it.
     In truth, all the trees are aflame with starlight,
     all the boulders warm-bosomed and inviting:

     we need only the eyes to see it.

Here

Here, in the wild, where there's almost no chance
of another human stopping through,
where there's no hopping round
patterns of perception or acceptance,

my little cells uncoil like June cactus buds,
my ticking brain unwinds to silence,
my chest splits to let my heart out for a walk:
things become the softness they rightly are.

This wall of mountain, with no edges, holds me.
This rock in my palm also wears a delicate skin.
The air and the angels spread their silken touch
over all of this place: lighter than mist, finer than feathers.

Whatever you have suffered,
whatever low roads you have trod,
this is where you must stop and be broken
open in rich contradiction:

       savoring the deep peace possible now,
       longing for the untold freedom of hereafter.

CALL

Invitation

You've swept the floor, incensed the air,
set and lit the candles, laid out the stones, poured the water.
You've emptied your mind and unwrapped your heart.

You've thrown a party for the gods;

and just before the first guest arrives, the icy spear
of desperation shoots up your back column, tries to topple
your expectant pose, threatens to call the whole thing off.

If you spoke now, it would be a voice outgrown long ago.
If you opened your eyes, the rocks would seem cold, the candles agasp,
the water hushed, the room cramped and foolish.

There are many painful ways to sit in waiting;

most lead merely to other, further waiting.
But if you can glimpse the blossoms on the still bare branches,
if you can taste the plums while it's yet winter,
if there's an unshakeable bliss in your aloneness,

the spear melts and rinses your bones,
the stones breathe a deep heat through your toes,
the waters hum and wet your throat with song,
the candle flame pulls you up in its dripping undulation,

the shadows wrap you in their wings and whisper their secrets;

and the deities drop in like happy rain on the roof,
enter your circle in smiles, open your fine laid gifts
and leave you their particular kiss:
flowered on your brow or ringing on your lips.

Examen

If,
one day,
what appears
in the morning mirror
is somehow
not the sum
of your experiences
lumped neatly
into textured cheeks
and wised eyes;
if, in fact,
you don't even fully
recognize
all the folds
and glimmers
painted in the glass
as you,
what terror
or delight
might seize you
standing there
in your nakedness
and brokenness?

Could you
perhaps
peel yourself away
from that lost form,
stop its panicked breath,
let it die
right there
propped on tired feet,
surrounded by
the brushes and towels,

spotlit by a grimy bulb:
body and reflection
snuffed out together
like fallen lovers?

And,
in that dying,
in that fresh stepping out,
could you
and would you
reinhabit yourself,
reimagine everything,
kindle a new flame
in your cells,
feel a flight rising
in your breast,
know your feet once more
as sure, steady, directed,
see your eyes as if newborn:
wide, gazing,
rapt with presence
and wonder
and a pure fury?

Father & Sun

How is it we've become afraid to call you by name
as the ancients did so liberally?:
> O Golden One
> O Faithful Fire
> O Glorious, Blinding Splendor
> O Perfect Father Of All

You stream over and through all this, and do not diminish;
in your light, there's nothing withheld, nothing held bound in judgments.

In winter, I drink you in like purple cactus catching rain,
their thorned bodies splayed wide to land each fat kiss.

In days clouded over, I mimic that timidness, that veiling of the face.

And when you burn through—a smile none could turn their back to—
even my bitter clunky parts raise their eyes to your beaming gaze.

I'm standing now amidst this patchwork crusted snow,
this moistened sand, these new washed stones;

rooted loosely in this pebbled soil   for as long a pause as
these hurried hind legs can manage.

Inside this snug black-bouldered canyon—holy of holies—
a secret dark cleft in my mother's curved body,

> I've propped open my many cloaks
> to your naked light come close.

And you beguile me to stay on here:
to perch and rest upon these massive stones,

to feel the canyon fill with falling light
at sunset's final surge,

to settle in among the deep-throated coos of owls
nestled in the woody fingers of this lava-walled sanctuary.

In the purr of that owl talk run through my hair
and the thick between-calls silences rubbed along my temples,

something slides within my breast,
some frozen thing I cannot name

and could not thaw now cleaves its outer layer clean—
the melt drips from my middle like fresh-formed tears;

              and everything I've carried here
              is released into your care.

There's no one about, not a single soft-skinned two-legger hunkered near,
but I've never felt such belonging, never so accompanied

as I rise off the rocks and drift through the golden-hair grasses:

headed home to a waiting woman, two children alive like wildfire,
our gathering table, our bed of stars;

knowing this old healing code is always
quietly revealing itself in new configurations

if I only step into the folds of Earth's soft openings,

              stand bare in the spotlight
              of Sun's unflinching grin.

Service

How many of us have truly asked
Earth (the larger us) how best to serve her,

    and then sat long enough
        to feel her hand on our cheek,
          her breath in our ear,
            her unhurried response:

              Of your many faces,
              which will you wear today?
              For your eyes can entice
              the trees and brittle grasses
              to a watchfulness and caress
              or draw out their scowl and scratch.

        And when we pull our grief
      out of our belly like rotted roots,
    we can shatter it all to dust and pieces
  we'll be forever collecting again,

or lay it softly on the flame
    in the center of things,
allow its quick transfiguring, its sizzling tears and searing heat;
let it cook the meat of an unbred nourishment—
one *enjoyed* more than defended, just as Earth can be.

For she's telling us and telling us
    in so many languages,
sunrise and windstorm,
    in the elegant phrasing of
unrelenting cricket song,
snow curtains pillowing the meadows,
the flapping crescendo of starling nation's get up and go,

in the arresting statement of
a silver-backed sliver moon,
a twin-pole fir stretched fluently from one source;

(such gifts, doing all this
among us so plain)

reminding us that	*You needn't labor to be so mighty;*
nearly scolding us to	*Take pleasure without struggle;*
pleading for us to	*Just praise something;*
calling us to	*Love me back just a little.*

Awake

Once again, we've survived the winter;
    this time, knowing more, it was less
        an endurance test than a welcome rest:

        the dark a friendly wilderness,
    the cold air a second skin
wrapping us in its strong hold.

And, by the fire, sleep came easy,
    dreams building in an outer womb—
        like seeds in black earth preparing for springtime,
          stars in dark space readying their shine.

        When the buds break forth this year,
    when the leaves let go their wrappings,
couldn't the total fragrance, brewed just so,

quite overcome our countless mishaps, wash it all clean—
    our blood and the waters—throw us into a quickened
        rhythm, lift us from weighty negotiations of soul or sale,
          wake us from the dark trance of light-mongers.

        Today, now, let us this once not desert but attend the birth
    of the tender, unfledged visions given under winter's thick cloak
and tended by inner elves who slip sprightly from the body

and work quickly and quietly under the moon:
    like grounded stars, like seeds afloat and fleet,
        rubbing sticks and whooshing breath,

        the flames of a new way lifting in dance,
    reaching their palms up and whipping their hips round
before we have a chance to think.

Unnaming

You can scrub and scrub every surface of the house
without any sense of a cleansing.

You can sort and store all your papers
and still feel a relentless buzz pounding down like a herd of crazed hoofs.

You could be given giant orange moons above your yard night upon night
and deny your eyes a clearing or conversion.

You could even walk through waterfalls
and not be flushed fresh, clutching your hurts close to your breast.

You can live for years standing at the threshold of your life
and never unpeel your coat or uncase your feet,

your heart's fire long gone to cold coals.

In your youth, didn't you sink into your dreams with abandon?
Wasn't it your animal voice sailing in the whipping wind?
Did not a tireless stride live in your scuffed boots?
Were you not keenly aware of prodigious angels perched nightly upon your bedposts?

Now you've built a wall of pegs to hang each thing in place.

But somewhere in your carefully crafted story,
there's a space where you stroll a flowered field without naming anything,
where the conversations you desire don't arrive in the post box or phone receiver,
where the shape of your melody is as easily made as feral laughter.

We've foolishly fought the river's unfailing sweep for some time now.
Despite us, the clouds keep coming—clear-bodied as children—

coax us to release our grip on their goodness and allow their watering
of all the harvests waiting in the black earth.

Opening

I have cut off
my hair.

I have sent my clothes out
to walk about
on new bodies.

I have asked the television
to flash and drone
in another home.

I have set my books free
to speak
in strangers' minds.

The car is gone,
the furniture is sold,
the knives and dishes gifted on.

Even this pen
will soon dance
in another's fingers.

I have bid farewell
to my beloved family.

I am walking out of this house
into the wilderness.

I am stepping out of this body
into the abyss.

Now, show me,
God of all,

what this rapturous life
is all about.

Signs

I awoke to
a woodpecker tapping in the
cold stove, the clouded glass
his drum, calling in the dawn,
knowing the timbers
he'd thudded before would soon
sing with flame in the dark
iron box. I had even

asked for a sign,
some way to feel sure the arrow
of my body was aimed true
before flinging from
the bowstring
after sitting with the stones
in awakened repose
through many seasons.

There was a mouse, too,
newly expired,
laid out on a white napkin,
presented to me in
my daughter's still wild
and open hands.
He was magnificent in his way,
silver fur agleam and
jet eyes just closed—
his sorting and storing and tiny
plans all finished now.
Waking to it all, I set down

my insistent list and stood firm;
then opened wide the doors—
of the stove and the lodge—

and watched the woodpecker dart out,
turn and sail eastward,
then rise into the blue void.
My heart unfurled with his wings—
the bird body cruciform to the firmament—
and I began to step to
his lingering rhythm, my feet
light with the song

floating from the wood walls and
the chopped logs about to be burned
to a wispy afterlife of air
and prayer. All was
indeed well and would certainly
be well for many more
big entrances of Sun
and subtle mirrorings from Moon.

Education

We've got schedules that correspond not to Sun or seasons.

We've got schools and churches where the wild flame of Spirit is carefully snuffed out.

We've got mobile phones tucked where our medicines could be.

You'd be hard pressed to find a fairy tale or a poem dancing in our skulls.

All the melodies we recall were chiseled from the street, not whispered up from Earth.

There's not much that's really *real* in the learning of this world.

And the generation choosing body now is calling out our bluff,
wondering how we managed to muck it up this much.

I try to do my part to give my little star sprouts the good stuff:

teach them to walk out into the forest with an open plan,
to gather information with feet awakened to the land,

to forget their separateness in the glimmer of moving waters,

to stand unmoving among the sea of scaly trees, trying on
their open-fingered reaching and sprawling anchors,

to read the fluid, shifting scriptures of the clouds,
to bend an ear down to the wispy grasses and pick up their secret verses,

to fall into a web of dreams and travel it to the Center,

to be the clever spider there
reeling in its catch, feeding on the bigness of Things

and leave it all behind
to sail through space on a gleaming string of silk.

SPIRAL

Red-tailed Hawk

No matter how often you appear before me—
    perched solid in the branches
    or flown above, weightless and
open-armed—my body is newly jolted into joy

each time. I'm unprepared, my hair in tangles,
    my house scattered about; I have
    no table set, no offering in hand.
Yet you let me drop everything, stop utterly, while

the currents of my other life rush by, their weak pull
    revealed and shamed. With each
    succeeding visit, you stay on a
tad longer; our noble affair heats up and pulls me out

of a stale swirl of thought as self, lures me back into
    my sinewed limbs, my bony
    teeth, my claw-like ends.
I feel blessed, for certain, and what's more, I sense

my need of you, how necessary are these friendships
    beyond the common alliances,
    how you may have traveled
a long while for this reunion, heard my callings:

desperate or exalted. And now, you've come so
    close, I feel permitted to
    somehow flow into you,
to put on the sleekness of feathered shoulders,

the sharpness of telescope eyes, to know the sudden
    grace of lift-off—a salt pebble
    cast from curling sea spray—
to savor the rush of cool liquid air threaded and latticed

upon my skin. In such a perfect spell, my whole self
        is rinsed through
        and wrung out, hung
on the line and flapping: spent and contented.

Coyote Choir

For weeks, you've been camped in the arroyo bottom just below us,
    nestled in among the low junipers and colonizing elms.
It's only here and there I catch sight of you—just one —or a few—
    trotting across rocky hillsides or bounding through sandy clearings.

But each evening, you've sung the sun down together. I always listen —
    a wee devotion—and imagine the renegade choir gathering:
veterans and pups with fur matted and muffed, paws pushing out
    and haunches arching up, jaws yawning to life, throats coughing,

growling, clearing space for the voice.
    I don't suppose you need look west to know when the last ray has fallen
off the horizon; even eyes-shut, you likely feel the little change in light
    or air or mood that starts the nighttime spirits dancing.

The song opens and comes seemingly from everywhere, fills the sky
    and dances about the valley. I find such character in each voice,
each melodic line in its flips and glides and fine ornaments;
    my hungry ears gobble up every yip and yelp of the short, wild prayer;

and there's so much I'd like to know—even meet the group—
    but you're not much for fame or fans, I trust.

Yet it's clear you're watching us these years as you've come to sing
    at our ceremonies: matching otherworldly tones with my laboring wife
on the half-mooned night our son emerged, and keening long and low
    in the stormy midday when we let our dear unbodied one go.

And when we circle up to sing each week—a less polished or timely choir—
    your listening is palpable, our weird commitment interests you,
you grin to feel our lungs' modest reach. When we begin, I often close my eyes,
    tilt up my chin, and nearly sense my snout lengthen toward the stars,

my body reposition outside your den.

    I once stood a long while in gentle eyelock with you, lone scavenger—
the dry field between us—and reveled in your form: its ascetic grace,
    limbs lanky, nothing extra on the frame. I breathed my thanks, brother,

for all the music, all the magic in our arroyo.
    And friend, I hope your belly's always full, your bed soft and warm
under these lavish desert skies. Let us be good neighbors then:
    sharing space and bits of news by day and dilated dreams by night,

our families richly mingled by our common breath
                            and our dialogue of song.

Visitation

The silver dolphins came adorned in all the richness
of the moment, and on cue, as if we had called them to us,
or into form, by simply remembering
they often graced this shoreline with their presence.

I dreamed myself among them,
the water's cool bite skimming along my spine,
my rounded snout cutting the liquid skin
as I emerged—leaping skyward. I belonged, simply enough,

had a maritime tale or tune and could tell it,
could sing it, or not, in sweet freedom.

But that cannot be how it all goes
among the dolphins. They must ache and
hunger, break hearts and lose center: cry out
with certain fears in those long, cold miles of ocean.

I knew merely that they had visited—
silky forms rising and arcing in bold shimmers
of sea and sky and wholeness—
had wiped clean the careless babbling of beach squatters,

if just for one wind-swept, waves-blest breath.

Talking with Stones

Anywhere I go,
I know
there is a chosen stone
sitting,
blended into
the long wash of color,
yet quite distinct:
brilliant
and ringing.

When I find
the one—
with sides cut steep
or a belly rubbed smooth,
lucid or grainy,
planted or floating—
I can almost see
a heat rising
from its sculpted contours,
drawing me in.

And if I ask—
with no language—
to hold you
in my palm,
the generous yes
comes forth
fluently.
For this isn't
your first jaunt
through the air,
and in many lifetimes,
your firm face

has crystallized as
full faith, resisting nothing,
not even
my novice touch.

When I unearth
and lift you,
bright chip of rock,
I sense your
spinning,
your initial nausea.
I close my hand
around you softly,
old one,
and let you say
if you will stay with me
for an instant
or an age.

Either way,
I feel such *aliveness*
in even the smallest
or coldest
of stones: like
a pulsing heart
in my hand,
flooding me with
clean energy,
draining my poisons.

You might call
to go with me,
to sit upon

an altar
or by my head
at night
or give yourself
to the quiet vocation
of our garden wall
or just join
the prayerful pile
our children built.
Or else I'll feel
you speak your word
pointedly, choosing
fertile riverbed or
arid hillside
or the shaded
friendship of a tree
as home.

Whenever your sojourn
with me
is done and through,
I breathe my gratitude
upon your
aged slate brow
and set you down
or let you roll
from my fingers—
a quiet encore
of your large tumbles
and settlings—
and trust
our conversation
was blessed.

Mother Earth Ghazal

At dawn, you're cold and I stroke your back, waiting for a kiss.
You rise into fingertips of sunlight that graze your brow with kisses.

I comb your hair in quiet praise, a humble suitor among the many.
Your body warms and pulses, then spins away from my lost kiss.

I watch you stretch and wash your limbs; each long curve swells my longing.
Your hillside bosom and slope of thigh burn my mind, yet nay, not a kiss.

You call me to climb your cheek and bridge of nose up to the very tip
And linger there—four days at least—no food's embrace, no water's kiss.

I stand upon the peak, a naked beast between your eyes of moon and sun.
You watch me close and breathe on me, my skin awake with the air's wet kiss.

Timothy—you speak to me in the language of steady, saving rain—
Jump on my lips and lie down there. Your body laid out is a kiss.

I lower onto your soft ground, the tender pulp surges in certain bliss.
I give myself to you and you to me in that great mystic kiss.

Giant

As is usual, as is basic as bread, each week
I heed the call to abandon this whirring machinery,
to gather my essentials and head for the hills.
Like any of us who live from the unsullied energy
of hidden places, I follow the trim-cut paths
with a familiar pleasure, easing along their smooth,
sure way through the mountain's innards.

Seeking calm, seeking to shake off the static
collected along the denser, treeless trails of our age,
wanting to plant a prayer somewhere in Earth's good garden,
I do it all well enough over the steady miles,
in the ancient dance of feet in time: lifting, gliding, pressing.

Before long, my blood thumps in waves inside the throat,
my pores weep my waters in cooling slides down the spine,
my sore bits and cracked pieces begin to mend;
everything within sighs with river's easy sweep,
slows to breathe with leaves sipping and
streaming breeze like old men on their pipes.

Now, it's often I'm called a little deeper still:
I must cut loose from the scripted route—jag through brush
in fleet fits and starts—allow the push of instinct's firm,
weathered hand. And so it was today: I shinnied up
a slanted slope of continuous stone, my fragile self
held close to the jagged rock: needing hands and toes
and even knees to ascend and reach an unnamed perch.

There, then, my heart was completely alive again.
I raised my hands and was stretched up sudden
through the clouds along a blazing sunbeam.
In a flash, I was giant: towered above, pulled out huge,
someway everywhere at once.

And having glimpsed the world that way,
I've been a giant ever since, and all I'm meant to do is play:
cup the silver moon into my hands for a kiss,
splash joy in and out of dark oceans,
blow old fuzz and seeds from rising trees,
suck lovingly on fallen icebergs.

Fluency

In the effort to become more like water,
I've taken to walking the dried arroyos of New Mexico.
Gliding along their twisting, sandy trails,
following the water's worn tracks round trees and brush
                                        and endless rock,

my blood flushes itself through,
my spine rises back into an aery float,
my eyes moisten and relax their glare,
my fixed notions and fine judgments blur
                                        into the total.

The soft, pebbled sand lends my legs
a boyish bounce and the walking rather does itself—
fueled by the ghosted river current
still running strong between
                                        the shallow banks.

Sometimes, I'm sure I spot a flash of trout
just ahead wriggling its fins
or feel a misting rise off the grainy riverbed
                                        and fill my nose.

But the dryness offers its own comfort
and its truth—cracked and thirsting—
reminds me why I came and what I might
need carry home lest my skin turn pale and brittle,
                                        my air go stale.

Once, in a prairie land still full of voices,
where the plants and roots have never fallen silent,
I shook hands with a stooped, wizened Lakota grandma
at a feast. Her gnarled fingers curled round my hand
and the space between our palms

                                  glowed like fire.

She hardly grazed my skin; it was the gentlest of touches.
And yet my whole form felt embraced by her warmth,
a lightness rippled through as if I'd been dipped

                                  in a cool brook.

Life was there—full up and rushing!—and not held bound
but given so freely, I yearned to know what Source her cords

                                  led to and fed from.

Surely, she spoke to the waters at dawn, called on them,
her bucket bathing more a soaking in than a washing off.
Her coffee was seeped as precious medicine,
her food boiled in holy rain

                                  over a talking flame.

And her patchwork trailer house—with no TV or books—
was ever filled with fluid visitors—legged or winged, furred or scaled—
streaming in the bright doorway

                                  of the wood stove.

I know by now she's gone beyond, but sometimes, on my walks,
I find her shadow sitting beneath the knotted fingers
of a piñon pine. I unshoulder my pack and kneel; and when

                                  she's nodded me in,

I settle and offer her water. She breathes on it and sips
then gives it back, *Drink, grandson,* she tones.
And when I've swallowed and made my prayer
and tasted deep communion, she slips off again—around the bend
                                        into the rolling winds.

I leave some bread, a slice of fruit, a bite of chocolate,
a pinch of tobacco, and know we'll meet again—
in an arroyo bed or on a prairie bluff—and let our hands entwine;
and I'll learn anew to let my waters dance and sparkle long into the night,
however cold and arid
                            it may become.

Riverbank

I move through the
tall barren cottonwoods—
slender and sloping
like drip-dried candles
after night dances.

I crunch over branches
and brambles
to the river's edge.

The soft mud forgives
my feet, the still-green stalks
gleam before me. I pluck
a tiny belled blossom and
chew its sweetness.

I shed my slick-polished
city face. I breathe
an olden beauty
back into my bones.
My body unfolds, my skin sighs.

A snake slides out
from the brush,
its lined diamonds painted clean.
I do not retreat.
She has come for me.

She slithers in and bites
down deep, my flesh pierced,
my blood running along her curved tooth.

My animal-self rises
from its sleep. I am
returning to the one
wild land. I am becoming
human.

Breaking

At some point,
    even the mighty mountain's walls
        give way,

the regal elk
    runs rabid with thirst,

the elegant mother lacewing
    slips behind a leaf
        to shamefully consume her young.

There is a rising
    and a dying in every fire
        we feel and follow

sailing along our bit of river—
    where wide and wild
        and where thin and trickled.

As we blindly ford
    the twists and folds
        of current,

there's hardly a moment
    to wonder if the paddle will hold true
        or snap in two.

And, if it does split,
    the shapely head now splintered
        and bobbing behind,

are we meant to weep,
    or flee,

or raise our hands
        in solemn submission
                and gleeful freedom,

transfixed by each splash
        and flash
                of the waters

sliced by the bow
        and fanning open
                alongside our humble vessel?

KIN

Birthplace

Nearly every year, I return
to the eastern wetlands where I was born.
Even if I don't quite mean to, I am drawn back faithfully,
perhaps like sea turtles to their hatching shores.

When I arrive, the magnetism builds
and pulls me past the deadened domesticity,
beyond homes of wood and stone whose tired faces
long to be known or acknowledged.

I slip down into the trees
where I can breathe and see
and check the pulse of this place
that first heard my name.

It's those wild spots—hidden pockets
of teeming vitality—that hold the rest together,
that honor the original rhythms
not yet drowned in our concrete and control.

Whether it's the gurgles of clear twisting brook
or the entranced dance of overgrown grasses,
I borrow that freedom and feast
on that purity for a hallowed minute.

I have bounded along a thin path
cut into tall fields
that embrace like a woman's warm depths.

I have covered my face with running water
and felt my clay
reawaken to a more storied shape.

I have stood still beneath a dreamy oak leaf canopy
and been bolted awake
by a brace of cardinals ripping past:

two lucid red words
spoken into
the thick crush of green silence.

Miracle Lane

Suburban paradise, milk and honey for
A flock of freckled children: growing
And fighting and dreaming, always knowing
The feel of love, a thin breeze that teased our
Hair and grazed our limbs as we tore through
The house or ventured out into open
Woods, with and without coats. Even
The shadows and heartaches we sometimes knew
Appear sweetly in memory's gentle eye.

Could any pious priest or highest judge deny
The small miracle of seven mouths fed,
Seven sleeping fast upon their beds,
Seven who will always bless those wed
And those newborn, love those sick, carry those dead?

Pantoum of Julie Marie

She is the master of yes
Of fully open to the world
Her wide smile celebrates all that is
And loves all that is not

Fully open to the world
The rare blossom ashine on desert floor
Loving all, what is not hers to hold
She pulls to bosom, then sets it free

The rare blossom ashine on desert floor
Not schooled in fear or fortress
She pulls all to bosom, then sets it free
To ride the wind or anchor down

Not schooled in fear or fortress
Her children are the stars who sing all night
And ride the wind or anchor in the clouds
To hear a gentle song

Sung all night, her children are the stars
She called me to her side
To hear a gentle song
I took pause and then made haste

When she called me to her side
I felt my ears alive again
I took pause and then made haste
To kneel and kiss her soul

I felt my heart alive again
To smile and celebrate all that is
I kneeled and kissed her soul
She is the master of yes

Joyful Runner

You ran joyfully across the wide sky
Toward your mother's womb, spots of starlight
Glowing and fading beneath each pit-pat
Of your spirit feet, like jellyfish aflash
In the night ocean. You heard the drum
And began to dance in circles of Sun
And Moon who hung waiting for your first dawn.
Spiders pulled you in safely on a song.

In a few quick years, you've shed your infant self
And stand newborn, a vernal shoot in the swelled
Meadow of discovery. Go run and dance
Across the land, taste it all; abundance
Pours forth from every stone, every tree:
Each bloom, each fruit. Eat life ripe, juice so sweet.

Anointing

Three months after
you moved
from the perfect darkness
of womb water
into the invisible ocean
of air,
I marked your
already-blessed forehead
with the bright scarlet
blood
of your birth.

Your eyes
blazed with attention,
and your stout little
body
pulsed with energy,
sensing the invitation
to be its
own being.

My finger painted
a spiral
upon your brow,
so you would know
always
the flow of infinity,
and feel always
the subtle magic written
into Earth's continuous twirl:
she, a dancer floating
foot to foot
in a great arc about
our humming sun fire.

And yet,
this new freedom
was gently tempered
by your mother's arms
laced round your chest
in the silent prayer
of communion
and the unspeakable bond
sealed down deeper
than even
that shared blood,

in the unseen
wellspring
of all blood
where everything drinks
as easily
and boldly
as two newborn lips
pulling in
their first taste
of the warm
white milk.

New Year Dance

At the Pueblo dances, there's a chance
to feel fully alive and not so distanced from
the even rhythms and easy harmony
of Earth and Sun in conversation.
This winter, I stood in the steady wash
of rattles rolling and clicking: like turtles
in their great armor-laden waddle, nosing down
to the river with dignity and direction
at the dawn of a new year.
My eyes became soft and the clay walls
came forward, smoothed mud and
flecked hay gleaming, billowing like
the sleek flanks of a warm-breathed deer.

I held my infant son aloft—
creature of rhythm, faithful time-keeper—
his head anod to the beat and to the timeless
swirl within it. What might his life be like,
awake so early to the good way of things:
a heartfelt prayer, a giving over of body
and mind, an open channel from head to heaven?
And my daughter, crouched low in her
moccasin-clad feet, content beside
the legs of shawl-wrapped women.
She, of me, through spirit and water
thickened to blood; here, in Taos, for the first time,
feeling the clay of her inheritance,
her own complex clay knowing and being known
in that soft land beneath those towering, snowy peaks.

And then my wife sitting
under the wood arbor, eyes closed
and soul open to the song: the tones drawn out
like long plumes of smoke off the crude chimney pipes,
the voices mixing and cracking like cedar logs
becoming flame. Her breasts full of milk
and her heart full of so many things
and so many songs to keep it all aflow.
What more could I do for her
or for the world
than to see so deeply into these stepping men—
bare-chested and tailing fox pelts in the cold—
to honor their devotion, to give them my prayer,
just a drop of light, a modest sip
for any thirsting soul? And in giving,
and forgiving all smallnesses, theirs and mine,
I felt my old posture fall away into the restful earth
and another form rise: this time
not only uttering the truth, but shaped of it,
dancing as it round and round.

Golden Jubilee

Seasoned nuns rose
among the narrow pews
and whispered their vows once more.

Father smiled and signed the cross,
a fly buzzing halos
around his thick fingers.

Musicians spoke in strings
and skins and bells,
shifted our gears to a quieter pace.

First and second cousins stood
happily studying
fluid reflections of one another.

In the front row center—
Grandfather, *Dziadzi*, patriarch—
sat silent in his strength.

Stately, as fifty years before
when his daughter said,
"I'm listening to a call, I'm leaving home,
I'm following God."

And sixty-eight years ago too,
when Doc announced, "It's a girl!"
and he declared, "She's Veronica."

And so many times before
and there, then, at the church,
and inside us all, descendants,
inheritors of that aged grace.

As our Sister Clare stood upon
the altar, a bride again
to that invisible promise,

some wondered how
fifty years feels and tastes,
turned the number round in the mouth
and the mind.

Others sighed at time spun away,
blew the dust of a near thousand moons
off framed photos
hung upon the walls of their minds

and peered into
the black-and-white shadows
of who they forgot to become.

Until *Dziadzi* coughed,
and we attended to now,
kneeling before
the mysterious sacrament of family,

of our unspoken and unbroken
commitment, consanguine
and congregate, like happy tadpoles

shaking off loose bits of mud,
slipping into a cool pond,
chirping, "Amen, amen."

Buried Nails
for my father

Every detail
of that dark
day
is etched indelibly
in your memory.
He was coughing,
as he coughed
most mornings.
Clad yet in bathrobe,
your father was rushed
through the kitchen
and out the door
by your mother—
terror in her voice
and movements.
You four boys sat alone
at the table
paralyzed
for a wide moment.

At school,
you knew the truth
and rose wordlessly
from your seat
to meet Father Pacheco
in the hallway.
Your brothers too were
gathered from school
and you all sat together
with your now broken
mother
at the Martin home.

He was gone
and everything changed
forever.
How to become
a man
without a dad?
How to be
a dad
for three boys
when still a boy yourself?
How to ever stand
up again?
How to hold anyone
close?

You wept gently
and quietly
at the casket
and felt
a nail driven
deep
into the soft flesh
of your
childhood,
the unsullied pulp
now crushed
and splintered
around its gleaming
metal head.
There was
no blood,
but the icy burn
drilled and swelled
your breast.

You carried
an invisible
stigmata
through adolescence,
through marriage
and fatherhood,
into the office
and out on the athletic field,
day after day,
sometimes forgetting it
momentarily,
then abruptly
clutching your chest,
fingers feeling
for the bump
beneath the clumsily grown skin,
cradling the
only real keepsake
of his presence:
this emblem of departure,
of absence.

We,
your progeny,
each grew to manhood
and womanhood
despite your secret worry
that you would
interrupt our journeys,
would miss it all,
would leave in the night
with no farewell

and no preparation,
death sliding in silently
and suddenly
like the nail.

But,
you were always there,
and you are here,
alive
and learning to love,
your footsteps timid
on that bright path.
I am learning, too,
just as I learned well from you
the seduction of anger,
the small, sightless ways of fear.

When I finally
shed those ready masks
and stood
face-to-face
with a woman,
everything lifted
and lightened,
air warmed in my belly.
And I saw the tiny swelling
above her bosom,
the skin knotted
in a familiar topography,
calling for my touch.
Her dad left in the night,
after coughing and coughing,

back home in Japan,
with his ancestors,
beside the rice fields
whose stalks still dance
to his name.

I have visited both graves,
one in the desert,
the other on the coast.
Both have trees growing
beside them,
standing and loving
that place
when no one is there.
You, as she,
stayed away
for a long while,
harboring all you thought
and felt
far from the sun
and rain,
in caverns beneath
the nail
that broke the bone
of your ease.

Fifty years later,
you hunger
to know peace again,
to hold it holy in your hands
and bite into it gingerly,
to chew slowly on its
sublime goodness.
Your father,

with arms of sunshine
and rainfall,
has waited ages
to hold you again.
With a fingertip of moth's silk,
he longs
to dissolve the nail,
to touch your wound
into a flower.

ONE

Fireplace

I know a teacher, wise—
less from years than depth
and breadth of inner travel—his eyes
ever ablaze with spirits or closed deeply
to a welcoming darkness where he walks freely,
in other bodies even, flying or swimming
or thinning out to star gas, thickening
to stone. When he speaks to us,

it is often in translation,
scooping up a few syllables that hold
semblance to that vivid, kaleidoscopic truth
swirling about him. He said once, as I heard it,
that the highest human act is to kindle
and tend a fire—on the land or in the hearth—
to stand open before the elements and good presences,
to breathe softly into an offering,
to lay out the sticks and needles
like letters on a page—the spaces between
there for air to stream—
to talk to the logs, whiff their dry fragrance
and anticipate their full-flaming incense.

All this I do and find it truly is
an anchoring, firm and steady,
and a soaring, free and ready for each
new twist, new image that begins with
the seminal spark and magical catch of infant flame
rising in its own shape and character.
I must listen fixed at first,
discern if it needs fuel or breath
or simply space to find its way,
to eat up my sprinkled prayer and
lead us onward. Once you're alive and singing

your pops and cracks, whistles
and whispers, dearest Fire, the real gift
and the divine office is to hold your
presence in my center—just like a new babe—
to feed you, fan you, encourage your growth
or allow you proper rest.
And—like an old one—to honor your sanctity
as the night grows deep, to feed and fan
less insistently, and, when you crumble
to glowing coals, to crouch low and close
and lovingly await your parting wisdom,
your final warmth.

Singing Out

When I let go my hold on this comfortable rope,
when I shed the legions of ready reasons to clamp up tight,
when I walk out into the soft light alone and undone,

even the very first footfall is cushioned in petals of grace,
a dozen murmuring spirits clasp my hands and rub my back,
the sweetest lightning slices the clouds to pierce my skull top:

and then there is no more body there at all
to carry the perceived or predicted grief,
no shell to burrow away in.

If I just undress this silly personality,
charm it with wine and wit, expose the gleaming form
from beneath the heavy soiled layers,

this singing essence will rise up and leap out
to claim her proper names: truth and trust
and yes, yes.

Arroyo Roots

To truly live is to know somewhere, some swath of land,
        in all its fullness, and as only you can.
        And never have I known anywhere as I do
        this wild arroyo-carved valley who has called me
        into a wondrous brand of romance.

At daybreak, I stand upon this rocky hilltop and gaze out
        at whatever scene the desert light has painted into life.
        And nearly every day, I run the winding, sloping paths
        through the stark landscape and remember myself again.

Whatever happened the night before—whether the unmatched pleasure
        of watching my children trance dance and happy howl
        within the sure wings of Mama and Daddy,
        or the sleepless torture of mining dark tunnels of the mind—

        it's all laid out and set down in the honesty of dawn.

There's a basic comfort in handing the Earth whatever I carry:
        a father's brimming gratitude,
        a poet's untamed passion,
        a man's freely-shouldered burden,
        a desperate darkness clawing at the ribs.

And soon, it's all gone,
        and I'm pulled into the naked wonder of a body in motion,
        present to the loving and life-giving exchange
        between striding feet and the bare soil—a primal reciprocity—
        a way to rub Earth Mother's sore back,
        to feed Sun Father's belly fire; really, the absolute least
        we can do for all that is granted us.

For much is gifted, even in this rugged sky land:
        the summer cholla flame out in pink surges,
        the spring cedars shake loose their great yellow puffs,

the blue grama and green foxtail and wild hollyhocks
are ever sprouting up or seeding down or swaying about.

As I run, the grasshoppers pop
up to pull off impossible aerials,
the jackrabbits hop out and
streak 'cross the dusty fields,
the ravens circle and float
and spin in their morning swim.

And, when it comes, there's the novelty of chilled air
and misted mountaintops
and slick-painted river stones
and a sudden green groundcover
after a long awaited drizzle.

When we raised a mud hut out back overlooking all this,
pulling materials from the land's flesh,
I sensed the Spirits smile and cradle the
rounded sanctuary in their hands, breathe into
its clay walls and timbered top.

Now, before its fireplace—the black stove our devoted monk
prostrate upon the bare earthen floor—
we have a place to sing our thanks in voices clear like bells
and expel our ills in growls rough as wolves;
nothing need be hidden, nothing stuck in our blood
or buried in our bones; we somehow portal out
of our pain-soaked forms and make ourselves afresh
of water's fluent slide and air's easy dance,

and then are ready to stand again on this good land:
not crushing the dirt beneath any weighty agendas
but cupping and caressing it with our foot soles
like a child's tender face or a grandma's heirloom grace.

Mountain Temple

This: this white-pillared, golden-domed aspen temple—
          with no doors or walls—
in fluid motion—in naked dialogue with sky and elements—
is why you'll find me less and less
          among the throngs of folks.

There are too many presences of more interest
for me to stay stuck in the paltry conversations
          possible on our cluttered corners
and in our altar-less edifices: our energies thick clouded
          and voices quick frenzied in aimless trots.

No, let me sit before a lichen-spotted rock who has sat through countless journeys:
          been buried years in ice, hurled through the heavens,
engulfed by searing, endless fire, possessed by forest fairies.
He is one to visit in these woods,
          to greet with a gift and stay near for a story.

And among more youthful spirits, let me feel a minute the dance
of sprightly mountain jays
          or the glide of silvered river trout
or the kingly strut of an antler-crowned moose
          crossing the ridge in royal hoofs.

That's high society for me, that's where the choicest class of beings mix.
Out here with the aspens and the firs—
          their gold and green each fuller sheened
by the kind reflection of the other,
          like a good marriage rekindled each year—

sitting in this lovely, lonely temple that you could never landscape or budget into being:
                              where the schedule's never fixed,
where the silence and the music gently breathe into each other,
where the soul knows exactly how to pray, as it always has,
                              in wild, unscripted thankfulness.

And beyond and because of all that, this is where
I *must* come to hear something worth holding dear:
                              a song, a poem
or feel something real enough to drink in:
                              a sudden misting of medicine
                              beaded over all my skin, soaking
                                                        in
                                                   slowly.

Trinity Well

It is said if you drink of its pristine waters in the month of June,
you will live the poet's life.

It is the home of *Bó Fhinn*, White Cow Goddess, patron of poetry,
her spirit flowing from that source through the River Boyne—
bridging worlds—packing the essence of things into our small languages.

Nine hazel trees stand watch above the mound that holds
the holy well; and the cows, a few indeed white,
hold vigil in the field beside the trickling river.

These days, you must gather several forms of blessing—
ancient and newfangled—before entering the estate's back gate
to approach that hallowed place.

I went through the forms and thus the gate—one June—
crossed the stone bridge that straddles the river's marshy beginnings.

There are many magic spots here on this wide Turtle Island,
but there, upon *Eire's* slim, stony, sea-wracked body,
I sensed my feet not so much discovering novelty
as recalling an old line along the land.

And I felt a bright cloud of witnesses peek out from the trees
and gasp in true wonderment; not so much that I had arrived
but that I might know a bit of the way of things:
that I would think to speak to them, and to the Sun,

and to the Goddess; then walk barefooted round the pool—
deiseal, sunwise—four times to open up the greater gate
before descending to the sandy lip, a grateful pilgrim bowing
at the edge of my next vast frontier.

There I prayed. There I laid gifts. There I spoke vows.
There I drank. There I was slain and risen again.
There was I newly formed and sealed as one true vessel.

And some day, when I see the well rising clear in his eyes,
I'll tell my son: Go. Make your pilgrimage.
Speak your promise in open air.
Give everything over and out to Earth.

For if you hold the precious things locked in,
it's not a life at all.
Even in these dense bodies, we are made of light
and are always being pulled back home.

Poetry

With the wild
　　　and impossible
　　　　　language of poetry,

you can snatch the moon
　　　and put it
　　　　　in your teacup.

Or, better yet,
　　　the moon can *be*
　　　　　your curved cup itself.

And isn't that
　　　how we plod
　　　　　through life, really,

sitting under the glowing
　　　moon, sipping hot tea,
　　　　　appreciating both tea and moon
　　　　　　　equally and fiercely;

the tea expected and anticipated
　　　as we filled the pot,
　　　　　lit the stove,
　　　　　　　spooned the leaves;

and the moon a surprise guest,
　　　filled and lit by another,
　　　　　sent to knock gently
　　　　　　　at the door of our awareness.

Then, suddenly,
　　　we break free of that presence
　　　　　through moon and tea

and recall our children sleeping
in the bedroom
and the garbage waiting
to be walked to the curb.

And, with the next sip,
we see our grandfather's hand
in ours clutching the cup,

and we notice the air
is growing cool these days,
we wonder how the aspens
feel in their limbs and at their roots.

It's like all that, poetry,
holding everything
in a golden phrase,

a lightning bolt
that pierces the mountainside
and ignites a hungry fire
to sweep through the weathered hills

with a new vision,
leaving rich black char everywhere,
fertile matter for the green trees
of further springtimes.

Poetry doesn't move along
in a line from *A* to *B*,
rather, it inflames *A* to leap up
and mate with *B*,

to swell her belly
        with the rounded, circling magic
            of deep living,

to create the precious little *c*
        upon whose singular face
            we all long to gaze.

Levity

Inside us each,
there lies a loaded seed
of distinct destiny—
waiting to be fed,
yearning to crack open and spread,
      like wings, into a life
not exactly chosen
but finally trusted.

For, it's sure
that the salmon of knowledge,
even upon
being hooked and cooked
by a clever hand,
      will still leap out
into the unknowing mouth
of just the right man.

When you cease
to battle
the unfolding years
and turning seasons,
you will float up from the fray—
not gone, not too soon departed—
just released,
      like a bright balloon,
freed to lift off the cold known road
and drift in spaces uncharted.

Gravity calls us all in
at the day's end.
But haven't you got
      lovely layered wings to extend
and winnow
before then?

Simple

To walk free along a high ridgeline,
to plunge into the smooth skin of sea,
to lie still on a fresh pallet of felled needles,
to stretch my heart over the long strobes of dawn light:

this is what this body was formed for,
this is the pure prayer of pleasure
that the Earth sings
into my simple and simpling ears.

Why would I choose anything other?
The mountain is never closed shut.
The waters are not too busy burdened.
The trees will not refuse me.
And the Sun reaches into my window each morning.

I stand and expand,
feel his warmth cup my face,
let my flesh enjoy its essential truth.
Give the body water and it gives back thanks.
Give it air and it breathes back grace.
Give it that sun fire, that fresh forging,
and it will slough off the worn cells
and bake the new self:

a pot, a bowl, a cup to hold
a drop of blessing, given or found,
and gifted back
to Earth's wide, warm lap.

Willful

When I am old,
I hope,
and breathe my last,
and my bones are
burned down
to powdery ash,
remember, my beloved,
that some part of me
will float from the fire
as a subtle warmth,

a secret self
emerging like ancient water
long cradled in stone,
a soft touch
left to linger awhile about
your aged face
then drift on into the
wholeness of air.
Yet, I think

I'll slip back into suchness
once or twice more,
hover in your threshold
as warmth,
rush into your lungs
and flutter your heart
like our first kiss revisited.
If, instead, my empty flesh
is laid inside the soil,

I'd like to dissolve
into the groundwaters,
achieve at last that flow
we reach for in our
stiff dancing and silly speaking
and holy longing.
Visit me then,
sweet one,

not at the grave
but by the river's edge
or before the quiet well
bubbling up fresh
through sand and stone.
Wash your face
with the coolness,
slick it on your eyes,
your ears, your lips.
Sign yourself truly

in the name of the Earth
and the Sun
and the moving Moon.
If you go first,
I'll do the same, of course,
my soul's daily drink
shared there among the thin willows,
the swooping hawks,
the kind water sprites
quick in my breast
and warm on my flesh.

Acknowledgments

Madi, my sweet Julie Marie: Our shared breath is my first source and food for my flame. My heart beats with the melody of your voice. Anjamora and Tadhg: May you know the Earth as a home teeming with song and warmed by story. Everything I have to give is yours. Mom and Dad: Thank you for life and the freedom to dream. Your steadfast love is ever a center point. John, Maureen, Brian, Anne: Our circle is beauteous and our bonds bridge all distances; we are limbs of the same body.

I send my love and thanks to all the bold, bright young men and women who journeyed with me in the Spoken Word Program at the Santa Fe Indian School. Together, we discovered a new way with spoken poetry rising from the timeless tradition of oral storytelling. I am wholeheartedly grateful to the Lannan Foundation for a generous residency that set me on the path of deepened commitment as a poet. And I offer my deep appreciation to Jason Kirkey for his faith in this collection and his fine work with design and other key elements of its presentation.

And in the more-than-human realms, I honor the voices of Nature and Spirit who have chanted the seeds of these poems into my inner ears and invited me to speak them forth. May my transcriptions and elaborations carry some small echoes of Truth.

About the Author

Timothy P. McLaughlin is a poet, spoken word artist, and teacher. He is the editor of the award-winning book *Walking on Earth and Touching the Sky: Poetry and Prose by Lakota Youth at Red Cloud Indian School* and the producer of a poetry album and a documentary film both titled *Moccasins and Microphones: Modern Native Storytelling through Performance Poetry*. McLaughlin received a Lannan Writing Residency Fellowship in 2011. He recites his poetry often in diverse settings and is dedicated to the sacredness and significance of moving poetic texts through the human voice. *Rooted & Risen* is his début collection of poems. McLaughlin lives in Santa Fe, New Mexico with his wife, Madi Sato, and their two children, Anjamora and Tadhg. Visit him online at TimothyPMcLaughlin.com.